HERALD OF THE AUTOCHTHONIC SPIRIT

For my children
Miranda, Cybelle, Max
And their mothers
Sally, Belle, Jocelyn, Lisa

by GREGORY CORSO

The Vestal Lady on Brattle
Gasoline
The Happy Birthday of Death
Long Live Man
Elegiac Feelings American
Herald of the Autochthonic Spirit

GREGORY CORSO
HERALD OF THE AUTOCHTHONIC SPIRIT

A NEW DIRECTIONS BOOK

Some of these poems first appeared in *Unmuzzled Ox*

Manufactured in the United States of America
First published clothbound and as New Directions Paperbook 522 in 1981
Published simultaneously in Canada by George J. McLeod, Ltd., Toronto

Library of Congress Cataloging in Publication Data
Corso, Gregory.
   Herald of the autochthonic spirit.
   (A New Directions Book)
   I. Title.
PS3505.O763H4   1981   811'.54   81–9486
ISBN 0–8112–0819–2   AACR2
ISBN 0–8112–0808–7 (pbk.)

New Directions Books are published for James Laughlin
by New Directions Publishing Corporation
80 Eighth Avenue, New York 10011

CONTENTS

COLUMBIA U POESY READING—1975

What a 16 years it's been
Since last sat I here
with the Trillings again seated
he older . . . sweetly sadder;
she broader . . . unmotherly still

with all my poetfriends
ex-wife & forever daughter
with all my hair
and broken nose
and teeth no longer there
and good ol Kerouacky . . . poofed into fat air
Eterne Spirit of the Age . . . a
Monumental loss . . . another angel
chased from the American door

And what the gains?
Al volleyed amongst Hindu gods
then traded them all for Buddha's no-god
A Guggenheim he got; an NBA award;
an elect of the Academy of Arts & Sciences;
and the New York Times paid him 400 dollars
for a poem he wrote about being mugged for 60 dollars
O blessed fortune! for his life
there is no thief

16 years ago we were put down
for being filthy beatnik sex commie dope fiends
Now—16 years later Allen's the respect of his elders
the love of his peers
and the adulation of millions of youth . . .
Peter has himself a girl so that he and Allen,
Hermes willing, might have a baby

1

He's also a farm and a tractor
and fields and fields of soybeans
Bill's ever Bill
even though he stopped drugging and smoking cigarettes
Me, I'm still considered an unwashed beatnik sex commie
       dope fiend
True, I don't bathe every day (deodorants kill
the natural redolence of the human form divine)
and sex, yes, I've made three fleshed angels in life;
and I'm as much a Communist as I am a Capitalist
i.e., I'm incapable of being either of 'em;
as for Dopey-poo, it be a poet's porogative

Dear Audience,
we early heads of present style & consciousness
(with Kerouac in spirit)
are the Daddies of the Age
16 years ago, born of ourselves,
ours was a history with a future
And from our Petroniusian view of society
a subterranean poesy of the streets
enhanced by the divine butcher: humor,
did climb the towers of the Big Lie
and boot the ivory apple-cart of tyrannical values
into illusory oblivion
without spilling a drop of blood
. . . blessed be Revolutionaries of the Spirit!

POEM

Summoned by the Muse
I expected the worst
Outside Her Sanctum Sanctorum
I paced up and down a pylon
of alabaster poets
known and unknown by name

2

and lauded and neglect of fame
I felt weak and afeared
and swore to myself:
"This is it! It's good-bye poetry for me!"
And the eyes of Southey
humbled me
into a nothingness
I braced myself
with self-assurances
muttering: "Being a poet
limits one's full potential;
I can ride Pegasus anytime I feel;
though my output has been of late
seldom and chance,
it's the being makes the poem
not the poem the being;
and besides, I long ago announced myself poet
long before the poem—"
The great Thothian doors opened
I beheld Her and exclaimed: "Ah, Miss God!"
She beckoned me sit upon a velvety gold cushion
I sat—and at Her swan-boned feet sat three:
Ganesha, Thoth, Hermes,
and over a pipe of Edgar Poe's skullen ash
they blew a firey diamond of Balbeckian hash
"O charming poet-stud whom I adore
my Nunzio Corso Gregorio
I twirl churingas, I sing,
you inspire the inspirer
for behold I am the Muse
and music is my sacrament
—I ask you, would you ever deny me?"
"Never!" I swore . . .
From Ganesha's curled trunk to Thoth's ibis beak
to Hermes' Praxitelesean nose She flecked cocaine
from the Dawnman's mirrory brain—

3

"Would you favor me your ear?"
"Happily so O sweet sister of sestinas"
"It's Emily, Emily D . . .
I implore you regard her chemicry
she who tested a liquor never brewed;
and Percy Bysshe, your beloved Shelley
who of laudanum did partake
. . . but I fear I'll embarass you
this question I would put to you . . ."
"O soul of Shakespeare, ask me, ask me anything . . ."
I could hear the silent laughter
of Her three messenger-boys
"I have no desire to upset you—"
"Ask; I shall answer"
"What thinkest thou the poppy?"
My silence seemed the lapse of a decade
The eyes of She and the three
were like death chills waved upon me
When I finally spoke I spoke a voice
old so old and far from the child I used to be
"Dear carefree girl of Homer, Madonna of Rimbaud;
morphia is poet-old,
an herbal emetic of oraclry,
an hallucinatory ichor divined by thee
as traditioned unto the bards of the Lake,
theirs and mine to use at liberty
but I am not free to be at such liberty;
the law has put its maw
into the poet's medicine cabinet
. . . I tell you, O sweet melancholy of Chatterton,
the forces of morality
and depresséd gangs of youth,
this God-sick age
and fields farmed by gangster farmers
prevents the poet ferret his mind
halts him his probe of the pain of life

. . . for consider, around that Lake
Coleridge and De Quincy were spared
the Eldorado Caddie connection men
and every other Puetro Rican mother's son
has his stash of laudanum
—for me there is no Xanadu"

"I ask you: Do you favor heroin more than you do me?"
The three each held a bloody needle
each needle a familiarity
"Was I with you when heroin was with you?"
A great reality overcame me
huge as death, indeed death—
The hash, an illusion, was in truth myrrh,
and the cocaine, illusion, was the white dust of Hermes'
        wings
Again Her awful tone:
        "Do you love drugs more than you love me?"
"I'm not ashamed!" I screamed
"You have butchered your spirit!" roared Ganesha
"Your pen is bloodied!" cawed the scribe Thoth
"You have failed to deliver the Message!" admonished
        Hermes
With tearful eyes I gazed into Her eyes and cried:
"I swear to you there is in me yet time
to run back through life and expiate
all that's been sadly done . . . sadly neglected . . ."

Seated on a cold park bench
I heard Her moan: "O Gregorio, Gregorio
you'll fail me, I know"

Walking away
a little old lady behind me
was singing: "True! True!"
"Not so!" rang the spirit, "Not so!"

SUNRISE

I am rich
I've used my blood
like an extravagance

An archetype of oralcry
whose silence
            smells of cheap wine
A poetman
become an olding messenger boy
O silver tongue of spiritus!
I whoop it up
        in all my wealth
                like Great Mercurio
                    twirling his white ribboned caduceus
                            in heavened air

Bathed & gowned
            by the Pigs of Prophecy
Asoak in a tub of soft flashes
            I step into talaria
And into my hand
            the twined winged wand was wound

I sat on the toilet of an old forgotten god
and divined a message thereon
I bring it to you
        in cupped hands

SUNSET

At the gate
  of the wood
    where the father
      nailed his antlers
        lies the snake Emeritus
          the Blue Stamp
            of the Virgin Wicce
              'pon its head

The alien son rubs against the tree
                lustily
And the She of Days
  holds a long Russian cigarette
             in her long hand
              humming a sutra

Falls the sun
       s l o w l y
      like
     a
       shot circle

RETURN

The days of my poems
were unlimited joys
of blue Phoenician sails
and Zeusian toys

Nights saw dawns
in the flash of my poems
the days were lit like books of matches
and the streets of my life
          were abound with marble fawns

I'd sing to one and all
Come if you will
to the other side of April
there where no blue yellow knew
where the Spring-born child froze
and no green grew

Love of life borne of dreams
          and statues in ruin
the fleshless arms of antique Greece
and the pale ink tan of painted poets
—an orphan child adopted by the Muse
led into April with nothing to lose

Extras came with every breath
all was gain
yet manhood seemed to elude
there was pain
and a semblance of death

The years awhile were poemless
Neither dreams nor ecru Greece

could induce what opiates
the more did reduce

Slowly I beheld the slow
demolition of the poet
I cried to Beauty
"Ill, I am ill"
and received no reply
Abandoned again
to that other side of April
I thought "Surely now I will die"

Asudden my hair turned white
Night passed day into night
All winter long I kept my blood in my veins
O wild wild horses!
yet held I the reins. . . .

Now as of old
the Sons of God shall come down
and make it with the Daughters of Men
now as of old
with their load of megagalactic semen

Let go O pen thy ink!
and lo! the page did fill
Spring came to the true side of April
I hailed "Here is your Spring Son!"
She cried "Well done . . . well done"

Of poesy and children have I sung
Father of both
The future is my past
the past my future

this from the present have I wrung
The days of my poems
again are the days of my joys
of blue Phoenician sails
and Zeusian toys

O stars of K.O.
never shall I know
      thy blessed knockout

I MET THIS GUY WHO DIED

For J.L.K.

We caroused
    did the bars
        became fast friends
He wanted me to tell him
    what poetry was
        I told him

Happy tipsy one night
I took him home to see my newborn child
A great sorrow overcame him
"O Gregory" he moaned
      "you brought up something to die"

EARLIEST MEMORY

What's the first thing you remember?
How old were you?
And at what age did you realize it?
Or had you always remembered it?

When I was two years old
a wondrous thing happened:
Bereft of the woman from whom I was born
I was given to a woman
whom I believed to be my real mother
A one-year-old foundling
I lived with her for a whole year
During that year I distinctly recall
sitting in a bathtub with her
In the unforgettable silence of nakedness we sat
facing one another
My eyes steadied upon the hair between her legs
which was half submerged in water

Thus a double source of birth
recall I
primordial and contemporary
Water & womb
I beheld
that from which we're born
abathed in that from which all life came

WHAT THE CHILD SEES

The child sees
the foolishness of age
in a lazy wiseman—
the knowing depth of the child's eyes
innocently contemptuous of the sight

He knows foolish abandon
when it sits beside him
—senses the neglected wisdom
the spiritus not present
and suffers the proximity
of the nullified moment

WISDOM

I feel there is an inherent ignorance in me
deep in my being
to the very core
I know its presence
by an unforgettable smell
          first experienced in childhood:
A nose clogged with blood
          mixed with the odor of an old man's belongings

FOR HOMER

There's rust on the old truths
—Ironclad clichés erode
New lies don't smell as nice
as new shoes
I've years of poems to type up
40 years of smoking to stop
I've no steady income
No home
And because my hands are autochthonic
I can never wash them enough
I feel dumb
I feel like an old mangy bull
crashing through the red rag
of an alcoholic day
Yet it's all so beautiful
isn't it?
How perfect the entire system of things
The human body
all in proportion to its form
Nothing useless
Truly as though a god had indeed warranted it so
And the sun for day the moon for night
And the grass the cow the milk
That we all in time die
You'd think there would be chaos
the futility of it all
But children are born
oft times spitting images of us
And the inequities
millions doled one
nilch for another
both in the same leaky lifeboat
I've no religion
and I'd as soon worship Hermes

And there is no tomorrow
there's only right here and now
you and whomever you're with
alive as always
and ever ignorant of that death you'll never know
And all's well that is done
A Hellene happiness pervades the peace
and the gift keeps on coming . . .
a work begun splendidly done
To see people aware & kind
at ease and contain'd of wonder
like the dreams of the blind
The heavens speak through our lips
All's caught what could not be found
All's brought what was left behind

FOR MIRANDA

My daughter
walks in grace
like a sharp New Yorker

I dream a dreamy child
in sandals of gold
walking the ramparts
of a Frankish tower

The Templar
kneeling by a streamlet
raises a handful of water
to his visor'd mouth
—there are white horses in Manhattan

THE LEAKY LIFEBOAT BOYS

Waiting for the world
not themselves to die
they scheme upon getting out of life alive
"Dead we couldn't make it out of Hoboken yet"

They don't trust death
"It's a gimmick" they say
fobbed on them
by that most unreliable of species, humankind

Humans unanimously agree
in time we all must die—
They disagree,
To them death's the oldest gossip in planet town

Their Christian parents believed
their deaths would get them out
There was Heaven there was Purgatory
even Hell
any one of the three spelled OUT
"Sheer lunacy!" these sons harped
"If you wanna get somewhere you get there alive
dead you're up shit's creek!"

These men are educated
enough to know
it be the living not the dead
that go
to all those dreamed of places
bound & unbound
say: distant Proxima Centuri via rocket hurl
or instant earth via out-the-window

These darling men ever getting older
are insufferably ass-bound
claiming the planet like the body
is a leaky lifeboat
and with a tinge of urgency, cry:
"It's bail out time, we gotta mutate!"

The desire to mutate mutates
'tis the fuel of evolution this desire
You see, it's not that they want to live forever
they believe they are forever
it's just the form they're in and on
that's deathable

They view the prophets of lift-off with
understandable envy
"Just looka Elijah! Mohammed! the others!
        they made the out-of-here alive!"

Of the three leaky lifeboat boys
one is of a considerate nature
. . . wondering how the planet as well
        can get out alive

HOW NOT TO DIE

Around people
if I feel I'm gonna die
I excuse myself
telling them "I gotta go!"
"Go where?" they wanna know
I don't answer
I just get outa there
away from them
because somehow
they sense something wrong
and never know what to do
it scares them such suddenness
How awful
to just sit there
and they asking:
"Are you okay?"
"Can we get you something?"
"Want to lie down?"
Ye gods! people!
who wants to die amongst people?!
Especially when they can't do shit
To the movies—to the movies
that's where I hurry to
when I feel I'm going to die
So far it's worked

17

THINKING CHINA

The tragedy of China is there is none
It was the year of the Rat
The Tyrone Power of China
thinking to address a wall
with calligraphs of mind
went to the dogs fast
—nobody's box office in China
His beautiful porcelain wife
became the mistress of the Minister of Eggs
His jade old sage of a father
took the road to Nanking
to relive its rape
His small gnarled quiet mother
wept like all great China
The son's One Man One Dragon proclamation
was old hat
None but the Rat of Heavenly Peace
ever thought to scratch the mind
            for China's latent individuality
This favored son this dopey husband this Tyrone Power
succeeded in bringing disgrace
            upon the entire family
And the newspapers branded him
            This Gang of One

THE PROGNOSTICATOR OF 64999

The year 65000 will be
as the first year
fraught with piteous mudmen
and rare German dogs
And the names of destroyed cities
shall be called by their rubble
in memory of their form
And the 300 year old carriers of corn
will rule the corn fields and
enslave the corn eaters
until the Festival of the 600th year

Nothing collects or is collected
—abundance with no space to storage it in
A natural rot rots everything
The putrification of stone is complete
And the second sun disappears
like a magic trick

ANCESTRY

Ganesha, oldest name of thee,
thou elephant on earth
patron of stolen money
so joyously seated with swished trunk
I know the message first divined in Sanskrit

Gilgamesh, second name of the scribe,
who lived the message
wrote the message
and delivered it
Thy baked language of cuneiform
tells of earliest hell
and bickering gods
O thou proto-Kerouac
and Enkidu, you proto-Cassidy
both on the unpaved road of antiquity
whose journey
from Uruk to the Old Man
who survived the Flood
did end in Uruk
you wearing a spotless white gown
as though you never left
The message of life told

Thoth, scribe of arithmetics, your palette
is carved upon my skin
—same paints, same brush
which did glyph the gods into three flags
and the strap of a sandal
into the symbol of life
I would jot down for all blessed things
the equal balance of heart and feather
on the scale of life

Moses, O Moses, thy
numerical letters
which did testify to the hand of men
as that which gave testament long before thee
by the deities of men
and the dispatchers thereof
Babel—the communicative air
all acrackle
in Geminian Time
O Great Messenger, who didst deliver a people

Hermes, you orphan god! Zeus &
Maya are no more . . . Behold Nunzio
his woolen petasus & sterling silver talaria
Apollo's lyre? Apollo's cows?
I take back all you took. . . .

INTER & OUTER RHYME

Last night was the nightest
The moon full-mooned a starless space
Sure as snow beneath snow is whitest
Shall the god surface the human face

YOUTHFUL RELIGIOUS EXPERIENCES

When I was five
I saw God in the sky
I was crossing a bridge
on my way to buy salt
and when I looked up
I saw a huge man
with white hair and beard
sitting at a desk of cloud
that had two gigantic books on it
one was black
the other white
Saturday I asked the priest
in the confessional box what it all meant
and he said:
"The black book is for all the bad you do
the white book for all the good
If the black book
at the end of your life
weighs more than the white book
you'll go to hell and burn forever!"
For weeks afterwards I assured myself
that buying salt was nothing bad—

When I was six
I saw a dead cat
I put a cross on it
and said a little prayer
When I told the Sunday school teacher
what I had done
she pulled my ears
and ordered me to go immediately
back to the dead cat
and take the cross off it

I love cats I've always loved cats
"But don't cats go to heaven?" I cried
"Thou shalt not worship false idols!" she replied—
I went back to the dead cat
it was gone
the cross remained
Fittingly so . . . that day the earth had died

When I was seven
I sat in church one Sunday
next to a fat little boy
I'd never seen before
He had a small glass elephant
cupped in his chubby hand
And it was during the raising
of the Eucharist
when he showed it to me
That's when it happened
I remember how fast it happened
He fainted
They carried him away
the glass elephant still in his hand
The part that scared me most
was when the two men who had carried him out
came back and sat beside me
one on each side of me
Was I next? I wondered
I who had seen the glass elephant?
I never saw that boy again
And to this very day
I cannot totally comprehend
what it all meant . . . if it meant anything at all

DEAR VILLON

Villon, how brotherly our similarities . . .
Orphans, altar boys attending the priest's skirt;
                    purpling the coffins

Thieves: you having stolen the Devil's Fart
And I stealing what was mine
(not because like our brother Kerouac said:
everything is mine because I am poor)
Rather: Nothing is mine, a Prince of Poetry
made to roam the outskirts of society
taking, if I needed a coat, what was taken
                    from the lamb

Killers: You killed the priest who slit your lip;
thus far in that respect I am unlike you
                    O thankfully so!

What sooty life, eh what, oh Villon?
An after-rain has laundr'd your day
blued is the white of it
Yet when O when
                    shall unsoiled navies
                    sail by again?

I know the same I knew before
Now I would less knowledge than more
for I know knowledge to be
such information as fattens memory . . .
aye, wisdom is a lean thing
for regard that head on his deathbed
hemlocking: "All I know is I know nothing"
You at least claimed to know everything
                    but yourself
And I claim to know all there is to know
                    in that there isn't that much to know

VERSE

I always believed freedom to be
a matter of individuality

Describe freedom
I'm not at liberty

The sidewalk isn't reality
Blockbusters demolish it

The individual is a pilgrim knight
Beware, beware a moon . . .

As all the world to boot the grapes come late—
Oh! and what has been done with George Sanders' things?
Are they trunked away in a cellar somewhere?
Who has his big-size suits? Goodwill? Salvation Army?
I dream'd going through his suitcases, his coats
        and flat-ass'd trousers

I allow you a day in 1936, say the fifth of May,
        complete with Yankee Clipper crossing the sky . . .
I dreamed a wet dream, whereby I came, and continued
        coming—
Hold o pen thy ink!

PROXIMITY

A star
is as far
as the eye
can see
and
as near
as my eye
is to me

MANY HAVE FALLEN

In 1958 I took to prophecy
the heaviest kind: Doomsday
It was announced in a frolicy poem called BOMB
and concluded like this:
Know that in the hearts of men to come
more bombs will be born
. . . yea, into our lives a bomb shall fall

Well, 20 years later
not one but 86 bombs, A-Bombs, have fallen
We bombed Utah, Nevada, New Mexico,
and all survived
. . . until two decades later
when the dead finally died

BOMBED TRAIN STATION, 80 KILLED

Bologna, Italy

Life has changed/*La Dolce Vita* has soured
and there's a big hole now
where children of vacation played
Life has become afraid of time and places
Who knows where or when
a suitcase will be laid?
Who knows what masks
bombers wear beneath their faces?

And in the world the world at large
there is talk soft talk of bombs
Carter talks like a monk whispering psalms
of bombing Russian bombs
of bombing the Russians in charge
even Brezhnev and the cars in his garage
And Russia threatens to bomb the U.S.
plus Carter, congress, the MX, the whole mess

And a bomb exploded somewhere
last year in the atmosphere
by someone nobody knows for sure
yet everybody suspects Israel and South Africa
I tell you the world has changed
Now the world believes a bomb
can knock at its door
that it happened not once
but many times before
I tell you bombs are real
and people, people are real
and both, people and bombs
are a terrible truth
not to be trusted

Whether it be a Hiroshima or a Bologna
the message is clear
Bombs EXPLODE
and people explode them
I tell you, hear!
the bomb is near
and it'll be too late
when it reaches your ear

How to stop its approach?
The poet can only try
And the Pope believes the path
to heaven is to die

FOR JOHN LENNON

A starthrower
    you'll be no more
        when tomorrow
            there'll close a door
                like an act of Jesus

It'll be neither day nor night
    when your hair ne'er white
        shall turn blonder than gold

Yea we'll walk the vast savannahs
    alongside your resurrection
        and with legs of spiritus
            we'll wade in the hossanahs
                of new water

THE GEOMETRICIAN OF MILANO

Luca Pacioli, what say you
there where triangles are more perfect
and the speed of the square
equal to the speed of the circle,
Is the sphere cubed?

The ear is faster than sound
sight faster than the eye
What's grabbed is faster than the hand
the body as fast as the bullet
both meet at the same place in time
The spirit is faster than Jesse Owens
Stupidity faster than wisdom
lack of thought faster than thought
The blank page of the poet
is like the slow broom of a janitor
sweeping the same floor for 25 years

That which needs energy to move is faster
than that which is moved upon
The road faster than the car
The ocean faster than the ship
The sky faster than the jet
And the tree, the tree is faster than the wind
in that the wind has to catch the tree

GERMAN VISITATIONS OF MUSIC MEN

1961

I walked that path of pyloned trees Beethoven walked
a grassy sky ahum with breeze and birds
arching melodiously towards the sunset

I sat where Wagner sang to his king
on the barber'd lawn amid manicured flowers
by the marble oval waters
clicking my tongue at swans

In the hallway where Mahler lived
I drank from my scarf-covered schnapps bottle
stamping my cold feet
and looked at the names on the door
The door opened before I could see
A lady in furs stood there motionless
"What floor did Mahler live on?" I asked
"Versteh nicht Englisch!" she screamed
I went out into the icy street
feeling a profound sadness of homelessness

I leaned against the back wall of the synagogue
where the young Bach was hired
to compose and play for the Jewish congregation
Here he wrote the *Magnificat*
on Jewish time

I walked, running a branch
along the picket fence
that surrounded Webern's house,
and stopped at the front porch door
where 16 years before
he came out and got shot dead
by an American soldier

For as long as I can remember
I always had the hots for Elizabeth Schwartzkopf
and can't for the life of me understand why
Though she'd a divine voice
it was something altogether else about her grabbed me
I'd fantasy living with her forever
having a most difficult time possessing her
and like a lusty satyr
I'd chase her gauze-clad body
thru private woods
from sunrise to sunset
until she'd drop, like a slow custard
utterly exhausted
chancing me to pounce upon her
and greedily bite her soft pink buttocks
together reveling in breathless grunts & giggles

Children children
don't you know
little Mozart has nowhere to go
this is so
though graves be many
he hasn't any

NEVERMORE BALTIMORE

O blessed dowser of lustration
drawn from waters where the discriminate ibis drink
raise the gold trinkets of Azteca
from the graves of the ladies of Castile
and bring it to Baltimore
to Sabbathai's music store
and there reclaim Apollo's plectrum
Pan's syrinx

Mrs. Poe, a singer,
died from a busted throat
And Mr. Poe
died from a drink
For every vote
the fop of Harvard
great-grandson of Calvert
tumbled the tumbler
with a twist of the wrist
and called the unnamed by name
With sand in his shoes he vomited on Maryland
and unable to call playmates
to come out and play
he summoned, instead, the moon for the coming Monday

The tarot lady in her costume store
is witness, can testify, saw the fall
of Satan's poet
in the gutter of Baltimore

She scryed her crystal
saw me leave the music store
the strings and pipes of dead gods under my arms
With an amethyst finger
she beckoned me enter the door

and take seat upon a triangular cushion
spiked to the floor
She knew
I celebrated my 38th year on Easter Sunday
a rare occasion indeed—
I heard tell of Sin and Nut
of Parsifal
and of which direction the eight wands flowed
And was shown
the child Poe holding a midget doll
"And this is the top hat he wore"
said she, twirling it
"Same hat outa which he plucked
the Mayor of Baltimore like a rabbit"
She plunked it upon my head
so big it covered my eyes
"You can't have it!" she yelled
and flung it over her shoulder into the pitch
"You would-be!" screeched she
"At least he knew a wicca from a wicce!"

WHEN A BOY . . .

When a boy
I monitored the stairs
altar'd the mass
flew the birds of New York City

And in summer camp
I kissed the moon
            in a barrel of rain

GETTING TO THE POEM

I have lived by the grace of Jews and girls
I have nothing
and am not wanting

I write poems from the spirit
for the spirit
and have everything

A poet's fate is by choice
I have chosen
and am well pleased

A drunk dreamer in reality
is an awful contradiction
Loved ones fall away from me
and I am become wanting

Self-diagnosis:
A penniless living legend
needs get the monies
or write more poems
or both
If you have a choice
between two things
and cannot decide
—take both
'Tis not right for me to be wanting

I take out my pen
I pee white gold
And on the wall
I write thereon:
It was there

always there
minutely contained
in a splayed hand

Outside
    a fallen swallow
        marks the Tuesday
O my heart! finally
    at long last
        I am at peace
The half-century war
    I hacked at
        like an Afric Bushman
            hacking bushmasters
                    is over

I will live
    and never know my death

THE DAY BEFORE THE PHENOMENON

Did you know
who I was
before I knew?

I knew you
after I asked—
Who am I?

Never did you tell me
who you were
I only learned to know
when I poem'd it so

And you
—is that when you knew too?

MONEY/LOVE

Truly money is a happiness
a false one
Yet it can spare the human soul
the cold lonely living death
        of the streets
It can comfort him with
            whatever has a price
It can help a blind man
            with anything but sight
and Love
Love is a luxury

The love one human has for another
        is heartfelt, without doubt
The love one has for money
        is unable to purchase love
The love one has for the God
        sensed by all humankind
        is unsure, by faith enjoined,
        An answer to the impermanence
                    of things and oneself—
Which love is the greater?
The first when it strikes
        the heart
The second when the heart is
        broken
The third when the first is maintained
        And the second is of no consequence

EYES

Blessèd be the bountiful emanations availed
      these eyes . . .
What was once Italian-wide
      has been prescribed the shades of age
And the coming of days
      have already gone by

I have seen
      come reality come dream come memory
all that I shall ever see
yet blessèd be the changing samenesses
tomorrow
      with its little satchel of wondrous strangenesses

Hallucinations will never bamboozle these eyes
—beauties and the joys of them
superimpose their truth upon all the lies

If never beneath all these eons of sky
a birth-splash of nebulae illume my eye
I still shall have anticipation
      a future to look forward to
I know that that which came first
      shall in spacetime come last
—between the vast off-far
      and the eye
      speeds the light of what used to be

A chemic change issues forth beauteous dilations
All's seen by deep hazel pools
And the setting sun's an illusion
its reality having set 8 minutes ago

—drained
                    pinned by the narcotic dwindle
I flash upon painful memory
—I am all that I shall ever be

Memory is another kind of eye
able to scan like a spotlight
across all the remembrances
Ah—these memories so natured like trees
forest what I never knew myself to be

A scryer of the divine speck
                    stuck in the muse's eye
having therefrom scryed
                    YHVH begoding Abraham
                    who in turn degoded Isthar
where all the disc-eyed Sumerians
                    lined the Euphrates & Tigris
                    to watch

A reverse oracle
who forecasts the Past
to whom the Morrow is historical
To whom this flesh fur feathered planet
                    shall bequeath the Future
                    a final whale catch heavy as the seas

I lift my eyes and see beyond the stink of madness
the self-same eyes
spraying great fumigations
And this dot of cosmosian light
by which all things and Being
                    were made finite and visible
                    —none shall remember
                    nor be remembered

Eyeless I see:
Love
And I did not know it was there
until it was there no longer

The true me
the one I couldn't see

THE MIRROR WITHIN

In introspect I see myself
dirty-white haired
with ruined face
teeth, eyes, and nose
left unrepaired
and neglect
Dressed in woodsy clothes
with Florsheim white shoes
I could look like a bum
or philosoph
—it all depended upon my having shaved or not

To see myself
like a battered Greek statue
slowly ruining away
yet always with the same sense and feel
I've always had
I see myself

AH . . . WELL

People . . . nobody loves them
not even people
Want of love
. . . no one owes anyone anything
Whosoever pays dues hasn't
(I know of no collector)
They pay themselves
Those who demand respect
are seldom deserving
—not to show disrespect is enough—
People love only themselves
and not too well
Love for another
either in passion or compassion
stems from the heart's desperate need
The universe is alone
and people are alone in it
The Pope doesn't really love me
nor I he
Christ, his invisible love
I knew for a lover too
People bring on fear and pity
I fear human fragility
I pity coolies of humility
It's always a bad day for someone
Pain, Death
The Big Lie of Life
The apothecarian earth blooms the poppy
at best

SPIRIT

Spirit
is Life
It flows thru
the death of me
endlessly
like a river
unafraid
of becoming
the sea

I GAVE AWAY . . .

I gave away the sky
along with all the stars planets moons
and as well the clouds and winds of weather
the formations of planes, the migration of birds . . .
"No way!" screamed the trees,
"Birds are ours when not in transit; you can't give it!"
So I gave away the trees
and the ground they inhabit
and all such things as grow & crawl upon it
"Hold on there!" tidaled the seas,
"Shores are ours, trees for ships for ship yards,
        ours! you can't give it!"
So I gave away the seas
and all things that swim them sail them . . .
"No way!" thundered the gods,
"All you gave is ours! We made it all, even the likes of you!"
And so I gave the gods away

GALACTIC BIRTH

The de-opiated body
steams on the basement floor
in the New York July

Its hand reaches for
delirium's magnum .44
and shoots its head off
over and over again
Bang! Pow! Born! Brains blown!
Ziiing! Blotout! Bloodbloom! Trainsthrown!

The billion'd cells
of this miserable meat-hunk
wire the brain
like an electrified cat
Guatemala bounces from cortex to cerebrum
Guatemala! Guatemala!
The stink of suffocated green
"No Mayans!" he screams
"I don't wanna see no Mayans!"

Again he knows the same green
the snake-priest in the grass knew
Again the obsidian knife
hovers over the fuming heart

A snapshot
shows him lying on the old floor
of an observatory:
a writhe of multi-cells
alleles and chromosomes

The mud-skinned astronomer sees
the birth of a crab-like nebulae
circa 1080 A.D.
slowly develop in a polaroid sky

IN PRAISE OF NEANDERTHAL MAN

In a birth old and horrendous
I heard in a basement in a dream
the birth-scream of mothers
bounce off the walls of sooty coves and bins

and saw there white-gowned doctors
yanking goat-legg'd infants
from out torturous vulvas
incessantly wheel'd in and out
by white-masked orderlies
all besplatter'd with blood & goat hair

and the nurses beneath each hood
choked in the thick air
piling the amputated legs
of this increate indecency
neatly
like cords of wood

Upon awakening
I flashed upon a photograph
seen long ago
in an old magazine
depicting all the bones
of millions of years ago
—ape deer aurochs bear
pony mammoth mastodon man—
all dumped in a common pit in a cave

And there were other photos
of other finds
Afric gorges Cretean wells Carib grottos
all revealing a common meal

eons of human skulls
with holes
skillfully flint-drilled by human hands
the brains long since sucked dry
like so many eggs

And more finds came to mind
from the tundras of the Neanderthaler
to the Caroline peaks of the Alpine
It is not known whether Neanderthal Man
ate of his own
or mated with those much taller
and together evolved into
great Paleolithian muralists
Yet unlike their brain-sucking forebears
and the soon to come Alpine eater of bears
they bound their dead with beast gut
from feet to head
lest the ghost escape
(first record of magic date)
and buried them beneath the ground
upon which they slept and ate

Know this about that hoary brutish
bow-legg'd miserable toiler
who to this day is deemed a stupid thing
unfit for survival
you who claim his seed died with him
nor ever did associate (much less copulate)
with such heir as Cro-Mag, son of bear
—to you I say Neanderthal
himself knew to sing
inventor of the churinga
(first musical instrument)
able to make the air ring
I say to you you can separate
the yolk from the white of the egg

yet without the one
the other is none
—so again unto you I say O thou bigot anthropology
deem not Sir Neanderthal a stupid thing
all milk and no cream
in his time
     throughout the world
         he was philosoph supreme

LOVEGLYPH

O Potter
who wheel'd the proto-egg
how so lovely a man you were
when so young a boy

And those hands!
how often in anatomical class
I'd fancy their divine rapes
whenever they rose to gesticulate
the air into pharaonic shapes

And all the years it took
to chip the god from your eyes
chip chip chip year after year
until the desired shape
like a ton of sun
Amon Amon
did finally materialize

DESTINY

They deliver the edicts of God
without delay
And are exempt from apprehension
from detention
And with their God-given
Petasus, Caduceus, and Talaria
ferry like bolts of lightning
unhindered between the tribunals
of Space & Time

The Messenger-Spirit
in human flesh
is assigned a dependable,
self-reliant, versatile,
thoroughly poet existence
upon its sojourn in life

It does not knock
or ring the bell
or telephone
When the Messenger-Spirit
comes to your door
though locked
It'll enter like an electric midwife
and deliver the message

There is no tell
throughout the ages
that a Messenger-Spirit
ever stumbled into darkness

LIABILITY

My "enemies" are by jealousy made
They await my "inevitable" fall
with cold patience

Like some blest thing
I survive the hazards of being me
Everywhere I walk is ill-carpeted
Bars are crowded with assassinaters
I order a drink and begin to fall apart
Envious eyes flash upon my fix
I speak the unspeakable

The bartender, a truncated tyrant,
is the creepiest of hypocrites
  Powerless in
  the sunshine
  he's Hitler
  in his dank dive
and I am waiting
for his digital axe
86

THE WHOLE MESS . . . ALMOST

I ran up six flights of stairs
to my small furnished room
opened the window
and began throwing out
those things most important in life

First to go, Truth, squealing like a fink:
"Don't! I'll tell awful things about you!"
"Oh yeah? Well, I've nothing to hide . . . OUT!"
Then went God, glowering & whimpering in amazement:
"It's not my fault! I'm not the cause of it all!" "OUT!"
Then Love, cooing bribes: "You'll never know impotency!
All the girls on *Vogue* covers, all yours!"
I pushed her fat ass out and screamed:
"You always end up a bummer!"
I picked up Faith Hope Charity
all three clinging together:
"Without us you'll surely die!"
"With you I'm going nuts! Goodbye!"

Then Beauty . . . ah, Beauty—
As I led her to the window
I told her: "You I loved best in life
. . . but you're a killer; Beauty kills!"
Not really meaning to drop her
I immediately ran downstairs
getting there just in time to catch her
"You saved me!" she cried
I put her down and told her: "Move on."

Went back up those six flights
went to the money
there was no money to throw out.
The only thing left in the room was Death
hiding beneath the kitchen sink:
"I'm not real!" It cried
"I'm just a rumor spread by life . . ."
Laughing I threw it out, kitchen sink and all
and suddenly realized Humor
was all that was left—
All I could do with Humor was to say:
"Out the window with the window!"

DAYDREAM

Parsley-mouthed Miss Christ
looms her hurricane cunt
across the sex-dark flats

The atomized Sphinx
with glassy expression, asks:
"What was Milwaukee?"

Zoom! there goes
the gay fuckerteer
chasing the tail of light

WHEN WE ALL . . .

For Spencer Smith who died

When we all wake up again
death will be undone
nor the stain of killed & killer men
remain in the wash of the sun

In winter we fell
tumbling
like two shot ducks
from the sky; a dream—

Your blue Aztec aeroplane
landed my infant son
and I
safely

I wept to hear your son
tell me
your Miami landing
had you die

I too am crashing
crashing
. . . Ah, Spring will
        bring a smooth landing

ALCHEMY

A bluebird
        alights upon a yellow chair
—Spring is here

FEELINGS ON GETTING OLDER

When I was young I knew
                but one Pope
                one President
                one Emperor of Japan
When I was young nobody ever grew old
                or died
The movie I saw when I was ten
                is an old movie now
                and all its stars
                are stars no more

It's happening . . . As I age
the celebrated unchanging faces of yesterday
                are changing drastically
Popes and Presidents come and go
                Rock stars too
So suddenly have matinee idols grown old
                And those starlets
                now grandmothering starlets
And as long as I live
                movie stars keep on dying

What to stem the tide?
Cease reading newspapers?
Cease myself?
Yes, when I was young
                the old always seemed old
                as though they were born that way
And the likes of Clark Gable Vivien Leigh
                seemed forever
Yes, now that I am older
                the old of my youth are dead
                and the young of my youth are old

Wasn't long ago
        in the company of peers
        poets and convicts
        I was the youngest for years
I entered prison the youngest and left the youngest
Of Ginsberg Kerouac Burroughs . . . the youngest
And I was young when I began to be the oldest
At Harvard a 23 year old amongst 20 year olds

Alive Kerouac was older than me
Now I'm a year older than he
and 15 years older than Christ
In the Catholic sense
        I am 15 years older than God
        and getting older

Women . . . the women of my youth!
To think that once I wanted to give undying
        love to the beauty & form
        of a lady of 40 in 1950
I beheld her recently she in her 70's
        in a long black dress
        her once magnificent ass
        all sunken flat!
How cruel the ephemera of fleshéd proportion
Poor Marilyn Monroe!
No Venus she
The mortal goddess
        is but a hairy bag of water
—and so are we all
And stone goddesses even with all their amputations
        maintain beauty in their ruin

Strange too:
When I was 20 my father was 40
And he looked & behaved like he did
            when I was 5 and he 25
And now that in 2 years I'll be 50
            a half century old!
            and he 70
it's me not him
            always getting & looking older
Yes, the old, if they live, remain old
but the young, the young never remain
. . . they're the stuff what becomes old

No, I don't know what it's like being old . . . yet
I've a wife in her early 20's
And I've a son just two and a half
In 20 years I'll be 70
She'll be in her early 40's
And he in his early 20's
And it'll be the year 2,000!
                and everybody will celebrate
                drink and love and have fun
                while me poor me
                will be even more toothless
                and bony-assed
                and inevitably stained with pee

And yet, yet shall planes crash
Popes, matinee idols, Presidents, yet shall they die
And somehow with all this oldingness
I see with vintage eyes, Life; Spiritus eterne!
With all the comings come
and all the goings gone

FOR LISA, 1

Your nightbody etched on the sheet
I smell your sleep & flow my hand
over the rumpled impression
& incant such things you'll never
know you being in the kitchen
feeding Orpheo granola & Curious George

Pythagoras warned people like you
to beware people like me
advising Clear the bedsheet
upon awakening! Shake away the imprint!
Trust not the handmaiden's hands!
The spouse is never 100 per cent!

Not me, he's not talking about me
your Gregory whom you so love
Never have I scryed darkly
o'er the sweet curled shadow
your sleep wove

FOR LISA, 2

I saw an angel today
without wings
with human smile
and nothing to say

POEM JOTTINGS IN THE EARLY MORN

With these hands
I'll make new
things for you, my children
your hands so young so true

Churn I'll churn
the zodiacal orb
of the Great Year
each eon to carry thee on
my progeny dear

Yearn I'll thee yearn
to return to yr primal sources
and there reclaim
all our natural losses—

        O what a heavy fall
        I'll have if I fall
        in all my light
        down ill-carpeted night

        I can see myself lastly leaving
        moving away from all I know

        And when I reach the Inevitable Door
        I'll stop, stand there,
        and turn to look once more
        upon all I know

        I can see myself comment
        before I leave forever:
        "Nowhere . . . it's been nowhere"—

Man is mystical
Woman magical—

    A free spirit
    is a divine
    fuck-up

Walks Tyrannosaurus like a man
in the monster night
To this beastkind am I related
—closer to it than the god
from whom we're created—

A GUIDE FOR MY INFANT SON

Simple perfection
Perfect simplicity
It's easy
like painting a flower
or
snapping it dead

HUNCH

Luck is of chance made
A lady, a beginner
Is Fortuna
A spin of the wheel
Either good or bad
Either win or lose
Fool's play! the game—

Blessed be the hunch
The hunch is not a gamble
A hunch is nothing to lose
To play one's hunch is to invariably win
Not to play one's hunch is opportunity missed
Hunch is *feeling*— prophetic
A hunch victorious hath engaged the future
To play another's hunch is to throw the dice
Another's hunch is another's feeling leaving you cold
The only hunch worth its worth is your own

Go rub a hunchback if you will
Look up the definition of "hinch"
                        while you're at it

As for me
        I've a hunch it's a cinch